A Mindful Makeover

A Mindful Makeover
The Key To Your Ideal Workplace

Renee Michelle Herskovitz

Mill City Press, Minneapolis

Copyright © 2016 by Renee Herskovitz

Mill City Press, Inc.
322 First Avenue N, 5th floor
Minneapolis, MN 55401
612.455.2293
www.millcitypublishing.com

All rights reserved. No part of this publication may be reproduced, stored in a retrieval system, or transmitted, in any form or by any means, electronic, mechanical, photocopying, recording, or otherwise, without the prior written permission of the author.

www.teammade.com

ISBN-13: 978-1-63413-938-0
LCCN: 2015920148

Edited by Emily Shetler
Cover Design by Rich Higgins
Photography by Laura Rae Photography
Typeset by Jaime Willems

Printed in the United States of America

For my Dad and Andi

CONTENTS

Chapter One: The "Perfect" Salon — 1
Chapter Two: The "Temporary" Salon — 9
Chapter Three: The First Video Shoot — 17
Chapter Four: Becoming an Artistic Director — 25
Chapter Five: Following My Intuition — 33
Chapter Six: Creating the Education Program — 43
Chapter Seven: Becoming Manager — 49
Chapter Eight: Challenges to the Education Program — 59
Chapter Nine: Staff Meetings — 63
Chapter Ten: Quarterly Reviews — 71
Chapter Eleven: Hearing vs. Listening — 79
Chapter Twelve: Acknowledgment — 85
Chapter Thirteen: Vision, Mission, and Values — 91
Chapter Fourteen: Leaving the Company — 99
Chapter Fifteen: New York City — 105
Chapter Sixteen: My New Client — 115
Chapter Seventeen: Return Home — 125

Staff Meeting Exercise — 66
Quarterly Review Exercise — 76
Exploratory Questions Exercise — 82
Acknowledgement Question Exercise — 88
Vision, Mission, Values Question Exercise — 93

PROLOGUE

The past two years have been busy for me, and they have been the most fulfilling, heartbreaking, and liberating years of my life. I left a stable and lucrative job, sold a house, moved to New York City, worked for a world-renowned salon, moved back to Minnesota from New York City, became a life coach, became self-employed, rebuilt my salon clientele, and created my company TEAM-MADE. Meanwhile, I've had to work through a few intense challenges in my personal life, while writing (and re-writing!) this book.

People think I am crazy for trying to juggle so many things, yet somehow I feel as if nothing out-of-the-ordinary is happening. For me, having a lot going on at the same time feels normal, because I try to listen to what my intuition tells me to do and I do it—even when I'm in the midst of something else.

"Why are you writing a book?" That's the question I have heard over and over again during the past year from co-workers, family members and friends.

Which naturally made me think, who am I to do this, after all? I've been a hairstylist for over 15 years and I feel very compelled to tell my story, though I'm not a writer. I've worked in a variety of different jobs within the industry: I've been a stylist, salon manager, educator, and set stylist. I've worked with some of the most well-known names in the industry. I've built and rebuilt clienteles in Minneapolis and New York City. As a manager, I helped turn a salon that was just so-so into projecting a million-dollars in sales for our fifth year. And now, I have added Certified Professional Coach and Energy Leadership Index Master Practitioner to my resumé.

Who I am is a stylist just like you, and all the experience I've had in our industry has led me to write this book. I have a story just like you; a story that I hope will resonate with you. What I have learned has changed my life. I've found a new way of thinking and gained a new perspective on living a more productive life, and, even more importantly, a much more positive life. I have come to realize that creating strong team culture within a salon is impossible without chemistry among team members—chemistry that comes from communication.

So why *would* I write a book?

It comes down to the fact that we are all searching for the same things in the workplace: freedom, independence, and *less drama*.

I want to share everything that I have learned by working in different capacities with a wide range of incredible people in our industry. I want you to know that it is possible to enjoy going to work every day because you enjoy being a part of a team with effective, inclusive leadership. It is not just my story—if you are a stylist, you have a similar one. Most of us have had success in our careers, and most of us have also experienced failure. I've included reflection questions to help lead you on your own path, and each of us will have a unique story to tell in the end.

I recommend answering the reflection questions while reading the book. Each set of questions relate to the theme of each section. When you answer them, don't judge your responses. Think about what you have gained from your experience, even if you didn't think so at the time. Use *this* perspective to guide your future journey and challenge yourself to adopt *new* perspectives. History doesn't have to repeat itself. Reflection can bring a new viewpoint to a situation, once we are removed from the emotions of it. Any new mindset we gain now will allow us to deal with situations in new ways in the future.

I wrote this book not only to tell my story of successes and failures and how they have influenced my growth, but also, it turns out, because the process of writing this book has been such a huge part of it. As I said, I am not a writer by profession, so the practice of staying positive and non-judgmental while imagining an audience reading what I have written has been the biggest challenge of all. I've had to shut off the part of my brain that is on constant repeat saying, "What are people going to think?"

That said, this book is truly for you; for you to reflect on your own experiences and give yourself the chance to choose your perspective on those experiences, which have gotten you to where you are in life.

Use the questions to discover what you already know to be true for yourself in the past, present, and future.

The only person who knows what is best for you is you; we must listen to and have compassion for our inner voices. We must judge each other less, disregard that voice telling us what we *think* others think of us, and learn to approach new ideas and questions that come up with curiosity instead of fear and judgment.

So on that note, enjoy your journey. I only ask that you read and reflect with an open mind, open heart, and open spirit.

Chapter One:
The "Perfect" Salon

My story begins in 1999 at a technical college in Eau Claire, Wisconsin. Right after I graduated from the cosmetology school, I moved to Minneapolis-St. Paul, Minnesota to begin my first job as a stylist. The salon was in the coolest, trendiest part of Minneapolis, and it was gorgeous: beautiful wood fixtures, textured terra cotta tile flooring. It was an expensive, high-end spa, where clients changed into luxurious robes and had a choice of cucumber water or wine. It even had top-of-the-line electric hydraulic chairs that you didn't have to pump up and down! I was so excited. When I got the job, it felt like salon heaven had opened up and accepted me right away. I was thrilled.

Little did I know that the "perfect job" was going to last for about twenty minutes.

I also had no idea at the time that this is what it always feels like. You think you have found THE place, the salon to beat all other salons; the perfect, busy salon with great people in a wonderful location. You walk in for your first day of work with pep in your step, go to set up your station and...it happens. You sense someone looking at you. You look up, and immediately have a silent face-off with The One: The Salon Veteran, the one who "knows" the most. She stares at you, unblinking. Then you see her look at her groupies. They give a subtle nod to one another. Yes, it's that nod. The nod that signals that as a group, through some sort of intra-salon ESP, they've just determined how long it will be before you quit or are fired.

Meanwhile, everyone else is standing back, taking note of what just happened. They're all calculating their own next moves. The manager is at the reception desk, observing it all, thinking, "Oh no, I thought it would be different this time. But here we go again."

There is one sigh of relief, though. It's coming from the stylist hired just before you. As soon as you arrive, it signals that she has just passed her own When-Will-She-Quit test. But here's where it gets interesting: rather than help welcome the newcomer, she is relieved because now she can join the Stare-Down Crew!

Why does this dance happen so often? I have seen it over and over again in so many salons, both in places where I worked and places where I taught. I have even been the leader of the Stare-Down Crew! In order to move past it, we need to examine the why behind this interaction. We need to see how we can come together by asking ourselves why we choose to put up walls rather than break them down.

Chapter One: The "Perfect" Salon

Think back to your first day at a new salon (or forward, if you are not in a salon yet). Imagine what it would have been like if everyone greeted you with an open heart and mind, free of judgment and agenda.

Describe how that first day looks to you:

How many times have you been the newbie in a salon?

How did it feel?

How were you expecting it to feel?

Oh—did I mention that I ended up getting fired twice from that "perfect" salon? Yes, twice. I had never been fired from a job, ever. I was proud of that fact because I had begun working at the generally irresponsible age of 14. The first firing came after I told a coworker that the owner had been gossiping about his stint in rehab. I believed it was information that should not have been discussed with clients (or in front of me, for that matter). When the owner found out I told the coworker, a flurry of screaming and swearing in a back hallway ensued.

 Owner: "I think you owe me an apology."

 Me: "I think it goes both ways."

 Owner: "This is my salon and I can do whatever the f#*& I want!"

 That was how he felt. So I was fired. I said "Fine," and walked away to get my things. He actually followed me, screaming about how he can do whatever he wants in his salon. I grabbed my things from my station, walked downstairs to try to get away from him and to say goodbye to my friends. He came right down after me, yelling "Get your s&#t! Get your s&#t and get out of here!" He kept screaming. It was so intense, I could only imagine my co-workers felt like I did: stunned, mortified, and probably terrified that the same scenario could happen to any one of them.

 I walked home. At the time I was living with my sister and her boyfriend only a mile from the salon. Being new in town, I was trying to save money to get my own apartment. Now what was I going to do? I stayed up late worrying, thinking "There is no way I am moving back to Eau Claire! I will find something." Prior to being hired at this salon, I had interviewed at another salon in town, which now became a possible destination. Unfortunately, it was within the five-mile radius of the non-compete contract I had agreed to sign. Five miles suddenly seemed a lot bigger than it had when I signed that piece of paper!

Luckily, it got better the next day. My boss' partner calmed things down, and I got a phone call asking me to come back. I wasn't sure I wanted to go back, but I knew I had to or else I'd have to move home—which was not happening. So, on we went. It was a strange relationship—I was still his assistant! We would joke about it and act like it had been funny, which felt surreal because it wasn't very funny to me. The undertone to every conversation was always a little like he was out to get me, and I was feeling as if I had just entered the twilight zone and wasn't sure what to make of it all. Was this how it was going to be from here on out? Were all salons this crazy and did everyone just deal with it?

Six months later all seemed to be well—other than our strange relationship, that is. I was no longer assisting him, and I was taking my own clients. I was building my business quickly and was among the best at generating retail sales.

Just as everything was going well, one day it was all over. I came into work on a normal day, and the owner came up to me and said, "We heard that you were planning an employee walk-out, so we have to let you go." It was that simple and bizarre.

And it was news to me! I was planning no such thing. A walk-out is every salon owner's nightmare, and I would have never done something like that. But he wouldn't believe me, so I was fired, one more time.

It was a painful time, however I learned some valuable lessons from it. The biggest lesson I learned was that running a business based on rumors that are in turn based on assumptions is an ineffective way to run a business. It is easy to lose employees with a lot of potential when you assume what they are thinking or doing, instead of communicating with them directly. This was the beginning of understanding the importance of the art of communication.

Describe how you react when someone makes an assumption about you:

When do you make an assumption about someone else?

What triggers you to make an assumption about someone else?

Chapter One: The "Perfect" Salon

Describe how you feel after making an assumption about someone else?

What could you do differently when you notice someone making an assumption about you?

What could you do differently when you notice yourself making an assumption about someone else?

Chapter Two:

The "Temporary" Salon

So much for the "perfect" job. The owner had now fired me twice. There I was, wondering, "Where am I going? Will I ever find another job?"

As I mentioned earlier, when I started working at salon #1, I signed a standard non-compete contract; after leaving, I could not work within five miles of that salon for a year. So I found a temporary place, until I could go back to a "real" salon. Why a "real" salon? Because the temporary one was in the worst place imaginable: The Mall of America.

"How can I build a clientele in a mall??" I asked myself. Yuck! All the crappy food, temptation everywhere to spend your whole paycheck, awful holiday parking. There was nothing cool about it. It was a total nightmare for a 21-year old. I was sure I would be there just long enough to get back into that coveted 5-mile radius. Yup, just one year.

What could possibly change in one year? As it turned out, everything could.

I began my second job wide-eyed and cocky. After all, I had now experienced "real" salon life. I had some clients, I wasn't fresh out of school anymore, and I knew what I was doing. In my mind I was unstoppable.

Salon #1 was a departmentalized salon: you either cut or colored hair. I chose to specialize in cutting, so I hadn't touched color for the entire first year on the floor as a stylist. All I had was my color knowledge from school, and in 1999, that wasn't much. So when it came time to take color clients, I would consult with a few senior stylists on formulations.

I would split my tips from my color clients with whatever senior stylist had helped me to formulate the color. It was important to me to show my coworkers how much the help meant to me. It built up some great relationships and increased mutual respect, but, as I'm sure you can guess, some other people became resentful.

What I know now is that this kind of interaction—the simple act of acknowledging a co-worker's contribution to any kind of success in the salon—would keep bringing both clients and employees back to the business, no matter what name was hanging over the front door.

List the ways you've shown appreciation towards other people this week:

Describe how you felt after that happened:

Chapter Two: The "Temporary" Salon

After I had worked in the new salon a few months and was settling into a routine, Alex began working in our salon. Alex was an artistic director and he traveled the country to teach stylists in salons that were under the umbrella of our company—*thousands* of salons. He taught many subjects, including technical haircutting, coloring, texture services, and business-building skills. Alex was moonlighting, creating technical training videos and taking clients in our salon when not traveling to teach others.

He and I did not get off to the best start. After all, now that there was someone new in the salon, I could officially join the Stare-Down Crew. I felt like my time had come. I had earned the right to be a *little* mean. Who did this guy think he was, anyway?

He had only been at the salon a few weeks, when I noticed he had borrowed the clippers from my station without asking. I marched right up to him, jerked them off his station with one clean swoop, and said in my best Mean Girl Voice:

"Next time you want to use something of mine, ASK."

His response? He just smiled. Didn't say a word. He stood there quietly, let me walk away, and then proceeded to act as if nothing had ever happened.

He wasn't avoiding me; he was just refusing to interact in the way that I expected. I thought he would fight back, like everyone else in my life would. I had no idea anyone could act this way, and it blew my mind.

I was in shock; his sweet smile and peaceful

demeanor put me at ease, and I felt comfortable enough to approach him to talk business. I wanted to discuss what it would take for me to become an artistic director, too. I had been harboring a secret desire to be in the group of people that traveled the country, educating stylists. The artistic directors seemed to have a lot of fun with their work and commanded a respect that I admired. When Alex walked into a salon, the whole room would change: He would have that huge smile that said "Hi" to everyone. How could you not want to be like him?

He kindly went over all of the things I would need to do: I had to learn and practice the foundation haircuts and color techniques the educators taught, know color formulation and product knowledge including our private-label styling products, and send in a video of me doing a color and haircut so they could judge my presentation and technical skills.

He made it clear that from there it would take about a year for me to get an interview. A year sounded fair to me. I had only been doing hair for just over a year, so I knew I had to have time to grow. Plus now that meant I could **procrastinate** for a year! Ahhhh... one of my favorite pastimes.

After that conversation, I began watching him even closer. I noticed how he spoke to his clients and the other team members in the salon. I have always been good at observing what others are doing and how it works for them; my trouble was applying what I had observed in others to my own life. I always thought I had to do things my own

Chapter Two: The "Temporary" Salon   13

way and to do something different. I did not yet realize that being kind, patient, and a good listener naturally looks good on everyone, in each person's unique way. It was authenticity I was feeling from Alex.

When do you feel you are being your most authentic self?

What do your surroundings look like when you feel this way?

When you are being authentic, describe how it feels to complete your responsibilities at work:

How do others respond to you when you are feeling authentic?

One day, I came into work just like every other day, and Alex asked me if I wanted to help out on a video shoot he was doing. The company was creating a series of training videos that were sent out to all of their salons to showcase new cutting and color techniques, and he was the lead stylist on this one. Of course, I jumped at the chance. I figured it was an easy gig and a simple way to impress him. All I had to do was style the hair after he had cut it, no problem.

Why did I feel so confident about this opportunity? Well, remember that first salon, the one I was fired from twice? Guess what I spent most of my time doing? Assisting and doing blowouts! Alex could not have picked a task better suited to my skill set at that time. When I was fired, I thought my world had crashed and burned, and I would have to work in a place I'd hate. I had no idea that just knowing how to do a great blow-dry would lead to great things.

This is the moment when I learned that all experiences, good *or* bad, are a learning opportunity. You never know when a disaster may take you to somewhere positive.

Describe a time you were able to showcase a talent:

Chapter Two: The "Temporary" Salon

How did you feel during that experience?

What changed for you after that experience?

Have you ever been close to achieving a goal and realized that it looks nothing like you thought it would when you started? You might even have gone in the complete opposite direction of where you had expected to go. This change of course may make you stop altogether and start something new; while other times you just go back to whatever it was you were doing before you set out to achieve the goal in the first place; making you feel stuck.

What I learned by utilizing my skills in a new way is that goals are changeable, and they should be. When I thought I was moving further away from my goals, I was actually moving closer to a different goal that was better than anything I could have initially imagined. Remaining open minded to different possibilities was key to finding success.

Chapter Three:

The First Video Shoot

The day of the video shoot came, and I got ready with care: I chose my outfit the night before, did my hair and makeup perfectly that morning, left the house early and got myself downtown. Little did I know, there were two intersections with identical street names: one on the east side of town and one on the west. And as hard as it is to believe, GPS was not around yet to help me out. I had to figure out where I was the old-fashioned way: park the car, get out, and ask for directions.

Suddenly, out of thin air, as I'm about to put change into the parking meter, hoping to find a kind soul to give me directions, there he was. Alex pulled up right alongside my car. He rolled down his window and said, "Hey Renee! What are you doing over here? Get in your car and follow me!"

To this day, that moment is like a dream to me. He turned up out of nowhere, right where I needed him to be. If I didn't believe before that moment that "things are meant to be," well, let's just say I do now. So, I got back into my car and followed him to the right location. And so began my first video shoot.

Who is someone that has helped shape who you are as a stylist?

What did he or she help you see in yourself?

Describe the moment you knew that he or she had ignited something for you:

What changed for you after that realization?

Chapter Three: The First Video Shoot

That day was also a lesson in putting myself in an uncomfortable situation in order to eventually get to a better place. If I had let my initial bad feelings from my first interaction with Alex get in my way, I never would have pursued the path to becoming an art director. If I hadn't pursued that path, I would not have found myself in the elusive "right place at the right time."

When have you "put yourself out there"?

What was the outcome?

What did you learn from the experience?

That said, it doesn't always work out perfectly. Sometimes we put ourselves out there and we don't get the response or the outcome for which we had hoped. However, I can say with absolute certainty that it is in those difficult times, the times I "fail," when I learn the most about myself.

If the experience in your previous answer was one that you believe was "failure," how could you reframe it to serve you better?

There I was in the "loft," a photo studio we used to do all the filming for technical training videos. I was overwhelmed with disbelief and excitement. How did I get here? I was just over a year out of school, on the set of a video shoot. It seemed impossible.

After getting used to the intense work over the course of a few hours, all of a sudden I noticed everyone's energy become just a little more tense. No one was talking, and everyone had his or her head down, getting work done quickly and efficiently. Everyone was on best behavior. What happened?

Chapter Three: The First Video Shoot

I heard the door to the loft open; a booming voice and loud, powerful laugh burst in. Who was THAT? I hadn't even met the person, but already that hearty laugh sounded as if it belonged to someone I wanted to meet. I also knew he was important, whoever he was. I looked around and saw that everyone else had a grinning face, too, but behind that grin was a touch of nervousness.

Around the corner he came, a grey-haired man in a gorgeous suit, with a great big smile on his face. The first thing I noted (and the one I will never forget) was that he looked every single person in the room in the eye and said "Hi!" as he passed. When he looked at me, asked my name, and shook my hand, I just about fell over. This obviously powerful man had the time and grace to look me straight in the eye and acknowledge my existence. I wanted to know who he was and what he was all about. That was the first time I met my future mentor and boss, Gordon Nelson.

That one meeting set me on a career trajectory I never expected in my wildest dreams. And I never would have gotten there if I hadn't been taught how to blow-dry at the salon that fired me. Twice.

Who is your mentor or role model?

What is it about him or her that you look up to?

What values do you share with your mentor?

The day of the video shoot changed everything for me. I had pushed myself outside of my comfort zone, and as a result, I met an incredible group of people who became my friends and collaborators. Through my new co-workers' professionalism and individual perspectives, I learned a more mature way of seeing things (most of the time anyway). Gordon would say all the right things just when I needed to hear them. He would show a lot of trust in my ability, which allowed me to try my best and to strive for better. When someone trusts you to do something, even if you do it in a way that is not exactly "the right way," and they still say "Great job!" it ignites something inside of us that wants to do better, wants to challenge ourselves to always be proud of what we accomplish.

Chapter Three: The First Video Shoot   23

When do you feel most inspired?

How does that aid in challenging or pushing you?

Chapter Four:
Becoming an Artistic Director

At that point, I was still the newbie at the salon. The next steps to becoming an artistic director came so fast that I didn't have time to focus on the details of what was happening at work. I remember believing that other people must have thought I was a suck-up, and that I was too young and new to become an artistic director; now I am not quite sure if those thoughts were what others were thinking or if it was all in my head.

And that's where it gets tricky: it's so easy to make up a story in our own head about what other people are thinking about us and how they are judging us. Then we act according to the made-up story, not reality. Isn't it funny how we can twist things around and do that to ourselves?

Describe an interaction in which you represented yourself in a way that did not align with your intention:

What was the result of that interaction?

Describe how that interaction made you feel:

What did you learn about yourself from that interaction?

If I succeeded in getting the artistic director position, it would mean a huge promotion. This fact did not sit well with the other staff members and my manager.

So I bet you can picture the reaction to the news that the newbie was on track to getting a coveted job and would be out of the salon traveling most of the time on

Chapter Four: Becoming an Artistic Director

the company's dime, all after being there for a only few months. I wasn't troubled only by the *actual* reaction of my coworkers, but also the story I was making up in my head about what they were thinking. One thing I knew for sure, though, was the one thing people kept repeating to me, "You're so new, how could you possibly be teaching?"

Teaching was where I could not fake it until I made it. I had to be precise about knowing the information I delivered in class. I spent hours reading color theory and technique out loud to myself in my apartment until it made sense. I brought in countless models to practice haircuts. Most of all I stayed observant at work and always tried to listen and ask questions.

Looking back, it all happened so fast. That was good, because between what I *imagined* other people were thinking and my own ability to find fault with myself, the pace kept me from becoming paralyzed with fear. Normally, I overthink every decision I make, replaying every possible outcome in my mind, always thinking I could have done better. I am my own worst critic.

When are you your own worst critic?

What is your inner voice telling you in that moment?

What is another thought you could have in that moment that would be more productive?

That feeling of intense pressure of time to complete a task has always propelled me forward. Instead of avoiding it, I push through it because I know that I can learn how to do anything—just in my own way. I have a lot of ideas constantly running through my head, so when I choose one to accomplish, I need to just do it fast and at full throttle, with no one in the way. When I act this way I often just come across as being pushy. I know that I must seem very annoying to other people! But if I don't move toward a goal in the way I need to, I get sidetracked and never finish. I haven't always been able to communicate that this is the way I work best. It's not easy to tell people that I'm very particular about how things are done. Being able to discuss this personality trait of mine has brought me closer to everyone in my personal life, and has spilled over

Chapter Four: Becoming an Artistic Director

into being more comfortable working with other people. Communication takes practice and constant work, just like any other part of our craft. Embarking on my journey to become an artistic director, I was just beginning to understand this concept.

One thing to know about me is that I have ADD. It gives me the sense, 24 hours a day, that I don't have the ability to be organized and get things done. ADD landed me in the separate, small class in school, you know the one where a few kids sit in an isolated little room, where everyone knows the kids in there are not as smart as the rest.

Well, that's what I thought, anyway. I have always felt like I can't be as successful as others because I will always be one step behind, in the little classroom of life. I feel as if my work is second to others who don't need to have tests read out loud to them or who can focus for more than 15 minutes at a time on one thing.

And I know that it's not just the ADD; we all have dreams, as well as the self-doubts. We need to begin to realize we are so much more, and have so much more to offer the world than what our past dictates. We need to allow ourselves to begin new paths, new visions of where our next journey will lead. Especially in the times we think we can't. When we think we are not good enough, or where there is pain from old problems, those are the moments we have the potential to see our true selves and realize what is possible.

What limiting thoughts do you have from your past, that contribute to your feelings about the present?

What effect do those feelings have on achieving your goals?

What is another way you could look at that limiting thought, that would serve you better?

Battling self-doubt is a constant struggle in attaining goals. You begin to have those self-doubts and worries, you may tell yourself, "I'm not good enough." And "Why am I doing this again?" You begin to feel the pain, nerves, and worries about what others may think. You second-guess yourself. Or, worst of all, someone you're counting on to help you through the project leaves you. You ask yourself: "What's next? What can I possibly do now?"

At times, that answer comes easy. We recalibrate,

Chapter Four: Becoming an Artistic Director 31

realign and restart. But more often, it's as if we get stuck in quicksand. In that moment, our only thoughts are delivered by a little voice in our head that tells us, "No, you can't do that! Why are you even trying?" We begin to feel the pressure building up and we become trapped; trapped in our own limiting thoughts of why we can't move on.

I have experienced both moments in my life. Times where I can just pick up and move on as if nothing happened, and others that are the exact opposite. It's awful. I wallow in self-pity, bury whatever project I was working on, and tell myself I'm not good enough to pick it back up and begin again.

Think about it: When we hear that little voice inside of us, telling us all of the things we cannot do and why we can't do them. Perhaps that voice is really revealing to us all of the many things we *can* do and have the choice *to* do, if we just look at it from another perspective?

During this time period, I learned to take that little voice of self-doubt and see it from another perspective. I just kept going forward, making my way toward my goal. I followed my gut and took on whatever came up. So, for the next eight or nine weeks, I ignored the fact that I was both young and a newcomer to the salon. I ignored any naysayers I came across. I just went for it.

What are some things in your life that you think hold you back?

What about them do you feel holds you back?

How could you reframe your thoughts about what holds you back?

How do you feel afterwards, now that you've changed that perspective?

What is one thing you could do this week to move one of these areas forward?

Chapter Five:
Following My Intuition

For five weeks, I traveled with a woman named Maria—she was one of the top artistic directors in the company. It was a time when I would learn about a lot more than just education and technique; it opened my eyes to who I wanted to be and what I wanted out of life.

Maria showed me how to be an effective teacher: critical but nice, strong but gentle, confident but not cocky. Most of all, I learned to never bluff when teaching. Stylists can tell if the person training them doesn't know their stuff. If I didn't know the answer, I learned I had to say so—and find out the answer from someone who did. I had many classes where I would be challenged, mostly because I was a 22-year-old and had only been doing hair about a year and a half at this point. What did I know? What the heck was I going to teach someone that had been doing hair for a long time, sometimes longer than I had been alive?

On my journey with Maria, I not only learned how to become an honest teacher, but she opened my world to the secrets of travel, food and great hotels. I will never forget the first time I ate a scallop. It was in Rhode Island at this little oceanside restaurant—I would have had no idea about where to eat in a strange town, but Maria always knew the best places to go. We sat down, and I had no clue what to order. She guided my choice, and I ended up with these little creamy things on my plate that were golden brown on the top, smooth and silky on the inside, and still had the taste of the ocean in them. I was in love. I knew I wanted to experience more of this: more traveling, more tasting, and more seeing new things.

Describe a time when you knew you wanted more of something:

What action did you take when you felt that intuition?

Describe a time when you felt familiar with something, someone, or someplace that was new to you:

Chapter Five: Following My Intuition

How do you feel it connects or could connect with your life?

When is another time you followed or sensed your intuition?

After being on the road for three or four months with Maria and other wonderful trainers, the thing I was working so hard toward came to pass: I was offered a full-time position on the artistic team. This meant that I would be traveling all over the country, educating stylists, just like I had been doing and loving. I would be back in my home salon only one week out of every month. It was everything I wanted right?

Well, when I was offered the position, the word that came out of my mouth was the one word I would never have expected, and the person doing the offering wasn't expecting it, either.

The answer was no.

How could I have just gone through all of that training and say no? What was I thinking? Well, I was learning to trust my gut, and something was telling me that this direction was not the right way to go. It was partially the travel; Spending so much time away from home and not being behind the chair worried me. And as I mentioned before, I get bored easily, and doing the same thing week after week—even if it was physically in different places—began to feel to redundant in my mind.

That could have been the end of the story. But to my surprise and disbelief, the following week they offered me a part-time position. YES! I replied yes! Yes! Yes! It meant I would travel one week a month, sometimes two, and work behind the chair the rest of the time. Perfect, just what I wanted.

I ended up doing this job for 10 years. It would be the first long stretch of time when I felt in the groove with something at work. I had a full book of clients when I was in my home salon, and then I would travel one to two weeks out of every month. I was flying all over the country, educating stylists on haircuts, color, texture services, business skills and products.

Anything our company offered as a service, the team and I would teach. I also became part of a small group of stylists that did hair for shows and photo shoots for the company. It allowed me to manifest everything I had begun to learn from Maria: traveling, tasting new food, and seeing new things. Plus I got to be in front of hundreds of people, educating and learning new technical skills from my teammates. It was a blast.

Chapter Five: Following My Intuition 37

Describe a time you were "in the groove":

What was it about you that made that happen?

What did your environment look/feel like?
(Yourself, people around you, location, sounds, smells...everything you remember.)

Over the course of the first four years as an artistic director, I was still taking clients in the same salon. And what about those coworkers who were not amused that I had gotten the big promotion? They were still not amused. And that included my manager. I tried to counteract the negative feelings by always sharing everything I learned with the rest of the group. I felt that if I was sharing information, how could anyone be angry?

Describe a time you chose a positive response over a negative one:

How did that outcome differ from choosing to meet negativity with negativity?

Describe how you feel when choosing positivity in the face of negativity:

Chapter Five: Following My Intuition

It was working fine, but then something else happened: I now had stylists coming to me with their work problems, looking to me as if I could make big changes to the salon since, in their minds, I had ties to upper management. As I'm sure you can imagine, this situation did not make for a good dynamic between my manager and me. Even so, I couldn't help but get more involved: I offered my free time to train new stylists and set up classes for the salon. I loved getting to see the difference I was making in the salon—it was very rewarding.

The thing was, it had the reverse affect on my manager. She became increasingly bitter and detached. I could feel her disapproving glances whenever I was helping someone out. I could never figure out why this didn't make her happy. I was taking some of the load off of her; why wouldn't she want someone to help?

She had been at the salon since it had opened, well over 10 years. The business had seen better days. It wasn't in terrible shape; it just wasn't hitting its potential. The biggest problem for the staff was that no one felt noticed or appreciated. There was no flexibility in her management style. She seemed to be resistant to change. It may have been that she was burned out, annoyed by my chomping at the bit, or just unnerved by the idea of change. But because that energy permeated the salon, it felt as if any single person's positive contribution didn't matter. The staff existed within individual bubbles of resentment and disengagement.

As an educator I was traveling around the country,

teaching other salons how to have great customer service and share ideas among their team. But in my own salon, that was not happening. How could I go around preaching what I wasn't practicing?

After spending too much time complaining—and listening to others complain—about the situation, I decided to do something about it. I was becoming more and more aware of my surroundings. I saw teams in sync in other salons, and also some teams that were so out of touch with each other that I felt the tension as soon as I walked in. I could see we were somewhere in the middle: The staff was a group of caring people who were working in a salon with wonderful potential, but the individual stylists were just not being heard, or even being seen as people with the ability to make a difference. Everyone was just an employee, a body to keep the numbers up.

At the time, it seemed to me that the only way to get our salon busy and successful was for me to become the leader myself. I had the experience from being in so many other salons and seeing what our potential could be, I thought I knew what it would take to make our team the best. So there I was, unconsciously building a real framework for our salon.

Chapter Five: Following My Intuition

Describe a time you didn't follow your intuition/gut:

How did that situation turn out?

What did you learn from not listening to your intuition?

Describe a time you followed your intuition:

How did the situation turn out?

What did you learn from listening to your intuition?

What keeps you from listening to it more?

What is it costing you to not listen to it more?

Chapter Six:
Creating the Education Program

Even though I wasn't a manager yet, I wanted to begin a solid education program for both our new hires and existing staff. Not just a series of one-off classes, as had been happening with no particular rhyme or reason. I knew I was not the only one in the salon with information to share; there were very experienced stylists with great technique who would be fantastic teachers. Not only did I personally want to learn more from them, it was a perfect way to get them involved and excited—and away from complaining in the staff room.

I knew a true training program would have a huge impact on both the new and old stylists. By that point I had a mentor, and I appreciated what he had done for me and how he continued to challenge me to be the best I could be. Why shouldn't we do the same and create mentors for the new staff? It would benefit the newbies, while simultaneously recognizing the skill and compassion of the senior staff.

I approached the manager with my mentoring and training idea, and she agreed to let me try it. So off I went, putting together a few basic classes. At the first class, only a few stylists showed up. We had never had any formal education classes before, and remember: no one was feeling as though any positive effort mattered.

Even though the reaction was lukewarm, I just kept going anyway. I kept holding classes. I had senior stylists try their hand at teaching, and each time more and more stylists would show up. I was so excited because we were making a difference.

Describe a time you took charge of a situation to implement a positive change:

What was the outcome?

What was the most important lesson you learned about yourself from that situation?

Chapter Six: Creating the Education Program

By the end of the first year we had a great educational system in place. We held classes once a month, with a choice of three separate days so the stylists could pick the day that worked best for them. We also had a full training program for new hires to get them in the swing of things before putting them on the floor. Everyone began to feel more connected, and I continued on.

At around the 18-month mark of implementing the training program, I began to feel like something could have been going better. I felt as though we kept getting to a great place, and then our momentum would just stop. Staff-room complaining would rear its ugly head, and everyone would become a little restless. As a team, we knew that something was not clicking, that something was holding us back. We were missing a crucial part of our communication system, but we didn't know what it was. Many of us would bring up this fact in meetings to try to figure out what was going on, only to get shut down by management or to have the conversation turn into an argument. We could not figure out how to communicate what we were feeling.

Over the next few months, I had many conversations with other team members about what we could do to change the environment in the salon. We would bring up our ideas for change to our manager and she would seem to like them, but the ideas never came to pass. This cycle would repeat over and over again, and nothing ever changed.

One day, I decided it was time to put myself out there and see where I could go. I knew that it was time: I put in a request to become manager. I wrote out what it was I wanted to do with reviews, meetings, and product knowledge classes. I described how I would do it, and what the desired outcome was—not just for myself, but also for everyone on the team. I gave copies to upper management, and then I waited.

And I kept waiting. Major employment shifts don't happen overnight, especially with someone who has been with a company for 10-plus years. So, I kept busy, taking note of the things I thought were problems, the things I would do differently, and the reactions of others to common challenging situations in the salon. I was trying to get a read on what stylists truly wanted and needed.

A few long months went by, then it happened: I received a call that the current manager had quit. The job was mine! The adrenaline rushed through me. Millions of thoughts ran through my mind about what I would change first.

How would you change or improve your surroundings if given the chance?

What would your role be in that change?

Chapter Six: Creating the Education Program

Describe how would it make a difference:

What could you do this week to begin that change?

On the eve of becoming manager, I was building on what I already knew about putting myself out there. I learned that sometimes, just the act of making myself do things that are initially uncomfortable can yield great growth and new results. Change can only come from trying new things.

Over time, I also learned not to judge other peoples' outward attitudes and actions. Just because the old manager seemed unhappy in her job, that didn't mean she was actually unhappy—I had no idea what was really going on in her life, both at work and outside of it. I learned that I needed to be more compassionate toward others and curious about why people act the way they do. Judgment can only impede communication.

Chapter Seven:
Becoming Manager

On my first day as manager, I walked into the salon full of confidence. It was a place at which I had been working now for six years. I had intention and a fierce sense of what needed to change. Little did I know I was about to eat a generous helping of humble pie. I had a lot to learn about myself in the next few years. Things I would despise, things I would learn to accept, and things I would love and want to share with others. I was walking into the rest of my life.

What do you feel when you are sure of something?

How does that feeling help you make a decision?

So there I was, all eyes on me. Everyone wondering, what is she going to do? And most important of all: Who is getting fired? I was not known for my sympathetic side, so there was a lot of discomfort in the room.

First order of business: Demanding a mandatory staff meeting, no excuses. At that meeting, which took place on my second day as manager, I began to tear apart the back room. It had been a storage haven of expired products, ex-employees' miscellaneous items and gigantic dust bunnies. "We need to clean this up!" I demanded, pointing my finger at everyone unfortunate enough to be in my path.

"You! Take this down to the trash."

"You! Help me organize these products."

"You! Tell everyone not doing anything to clean their stations."

Oh yes, I know. I know exactly how this makes me look. But that is really what I did. I thought my new position made me the leader—the one with all the power. And everyone was required to listen to my plan.

I was so lucky to have Christy as my assistant manager. She saved my behind time and time again. Christy was soft and kind, she would clean up after my verbal assaults. She made sure the stylists knew it was all coming from a good place, because it was. She always saw the good in me, even when she didn't agree with my actions. I learned so much from her.

Chapter Seven: Becoming Manager

Describe what a leader is:

Describe what a great leader is:

Describe the qualities that make you a great leader:

What can you do this week to continue the practice of being a great leader?

The first staff meeting was a blur. I went on and on about how things were going to be different now, how there were going to be rules...and consequences when people broke the rules.

I really don't remember if anyone else spoke at that meeting other than me. The air was so full of fear, anxiety, and disbelief. I can't imagine anyone would feel comfortable enough to raise a hand.

As I often said, "If you don't like the rules, you don't have to stay." And many didn't.

The changes were forced on them in a way that provided no room for them to feel supported in the change or their own personal growth, no place for them to feel safe or understood.

There is a big difference between *thinking* you are supporting someone, and that person *feeling* supported.

The first year went by in a flash. We lost stylists, but at the time I didn't pay much attention. I was so wrapped up in how I wanted things to look and be that it didn't matter who the team lost. If someone didn't agree with my vision, I did not care.

We established a new set of ground rules, but the education program remained intact. Actually, I think that was the only thing keeping most people there. I thought everyone respected me and would have followed me to the moon and back. Well, I suppose they all did what I said. Of course deep down, I knew they followed me out of fear, but it was working and so I just used it to my advantage. I didn't know how to do it any other way

Chapter Seven: Becoming Manager

What is one thing about yourself you would like to make a positive change around?

How would that create a positive change in your work environment?

What is one thing you can do this week to begin that change?

Let's discuss some of the important tasks that a manager has to do that I hated: fun stuff like inventory, cleaning (and assigning cleaning duties), and ordering supplies. I figured out a way to only do the things that pertained to my interests, as well as anything that would allow me to see what the staff was *not* doing. I loved running numbers on individual staff members to see what their statistics were for the week, as well as checking to see if they were doing what they said they were doing when I was out of town. I could also check to see if they were where they needed to be to get a raise, or if they were just coasting at the same level.

We had five levels of stylists, and they all had the ability to move up and raise their prices and commission depending on their numbers and return clients. I enjoyed seeing the changes in the salon numbers from years past compared to what we were doing at the time; it was a great ego booster. As I said, I liked things to be my way and be the only one who was right, and I loved looking at any statistics that would show me I was doing well. Everything else? It could go in a folder to be dealt with later, or I would pass it off to my trusty assistant Christy to do for me. She handled the boring stuff like notices for inventory or changing the front-of-salon signage for new promotions.

I also thought delegating tasks to all employees would be the key to happy stylists. The previous manager had tried to do everything herself, which she would do silently. Or else she would do things like passive-aggressively slam the laundry basket down in front of us instead of asking for help. So I figured if I assigned extra tasks to the staff, everyone would love it. I would tell them what to do, and presto! They are busy and can't be in the back room complaining. Most of what I did in the first year was the exact opposite of what the former manager had done. I figured that was the easiest way not to fail, right? I'm sure they were still complaining, but when I walked in it would stop. So if I didn't hear it, it wasn't there.

Chapter Seven: Becoming Manager

What is an area you excel in, that you would like someone to acknowledge at work?

Describe how would you feel if that was acknowledged:

Describe how that would that affect your level of engagement at work:

As the first year went by, I knew it wasn't perfect. I knew something was missing, but I couldn't put my finger on what was wrong. We just kept plugging through the days, and in time we whittled down to nine stylists; we had started with 15. I created a new rule that all stylists who weren't making the numbers they needed to be at their current price level had 60 days to get them there—*and* remain consistent—or else they would fall back to a lower level (which meant lowering pricing for services). I decided to implement this policy because the former manager would give employees raises not for better performance, but to stop them from leaving. As a result, I had high-level stylists with no clients, and that was not teaching anyone anything. Many of those original 15 stylists left due to this policy, either because it did not seem fair or they just felt bullied.

Of the nine stylists who remained, seven would come to be known as the Ride or Die team. They were the ones who would stick through anything. There were no ups or downs big enough to make them quit. I felt invincible with this team: They truly understood my vision for the salon. I, of course, thought that was all they needed.

Think of a time you were proud to belong to a team. Describe how it made you feel:

What was your contribution to that team's success?

Chapter Seven: Becoming Manager

Describe what a teammate is:

Describe what a great teammate is:

While everything seemed to be going great, there was still something missing. A soft alarm was going off in my head, and it made me feel as though I was just not paying close enough attention to something, but I wasn't sure what that was. "Eyes forward," I kept telling myself. "Don't get distracted."

Why did I think that being distracted was a bad thing? Why did I not want to listen to that voice in my head saying I needed to keep looking? I was not yet comfortable with listening to my own instincts that were saying that I was going in the wrong direction. I wanted to feel correct, in control, and in the lead at all times. What I have since learned is that we *need* to listen to that voice, the one telling us: "Hey you! Look over here!!" even if it feels wrong or uncomfortable. That is how you find your direction, and become a great leader in all aspects of your life.

Every day we make choices and decisions that affect our own lives. We are our own best leaders. And *as* leaders, we must start with discovering our own wants and needs before moving on to leading a group. How can we ask for what we want and need in a boss or teammate if we don't know what we want and need for ourselves? We can't get on the same page as the rest of the team if we don't even know where we want to end up, or how we plan on getting ourselves there.

What can you start doing today to lead yourself to your true potential?

Chapter Eight:
Challenges to the Education Program

Year two began with a rush of good energy, but it didn't take long for me to squander it. We had the team that would stand the test of time—Ride or Die, baby—and everyone was committed to training new stylists. Each employee would take on a lot of the day-to-day operations so that I could continue to travel once a month, confident that everything was under control. There was a strict protocol for my assistant to follow, so upon my return everything would be done and I could focus solely on my clients.

The education program I helped implement before becoming manager was still going strong. We were holding classes once a month, and senior stylists were helping out the new employees, getting them ready to go on the floor. However, after a few years of success, the program was starting to show its flaws. The group dynamics of the system we had set up were not working out—resentment had taken hold, and both stylists and newbies were unhappy. I had set everyone up for long-term failure, and I didn't even know what I had done.

Here's how I built up resentment in the salon: The stylists training the newbies did it out of the kindness of their hearts. They all knew it was an unpaid position, which shows just how committed they were to the salon. The mentor stylists would come in on their days off and work for free, training the new hires. This cycle would go on for about a month, until the new hires finished all of the model requirements to get on the floor. The program was also set up to see who could make it: could the new hires get models, be on time, and do a good job?

Using this program as a tool to see if someone could "make it" was not only poor judgment on my part for the success of the new hire, it also set the stylists up to feel let down.

When the new stylists would begin to feel as though they were being *tested* and not *taught*, they would become intimidated and sometimes not show up for class. You can imagine the attitude of the mentor stylist left standing there on what was supposed to be a day off, just looking at me. "Well, I guess they just couldn't hack it," I'd say.

I essentially pumped up the mentors by insulting the newbies, thinking I was somehow helping the mentors feel better about themselves. But, in reality, being disrespectful and judgmental toward fellow staff members just created room for massive resentment and left everyone feeling bitter and as if they were being treated unfairly.

So there I was, looking at my mentor stylists, opening the door to judgment and ushering it right in. My attitude made the mentors feel their time was being wasted because the new stylists "just couldn't hack it." But to the loyal stylists' credit, they kept plugging through, showing up for classes and training the new hires. Only now, I had placed a chip on their shoulders. My voice in their heads

Chapter Eight: Challenges to the Education Program 61

saying: "Can they hack it? Can they hack it?" turned good intentions into judgmental thoughts. Add in some of that silent killer—resentment—and you have the makings of an unsuccessful salon.

I am sure we lost a few great new stylists because they were too intimidated; real potential team members that, nurtured the right way, would have turned out to be great employees and busy stylists. But on we went.

What causes you to feel resentment at work?

How does that affect your performance?

Describe how could you communicate this to create a positive outcome:

The resentment grew from not communicating honestly and directly to both senior stylists and the newbies. In order to be a great at our craft, we have to first learn and understand cut and color techniques in order for our hands to create something beautiful. That was what I was trying to institute with the education program. But I failed to see the link between technique and communication. As stylists, we spend countless hours trying to educate ourselves on technique, business, and customer service, and usually come back to the same end result: Anxiety-filled hours, never achieving everything we hope to achieve. It is the lack of communication that keeps us trapped.

Understanding teammates and communication without judgment or intimidation is a key element of salon communication. Had I been able to communicate more clearly as a manager, we would not have built up resentment in the salon, and we would not have lost those stylists with great potential.

Chapter Nine:
Staff Meetings

By the end of the second year, I felt as though we had found our stride. We were hitting our top goals and setting new ones. For the most part, we were having a lot of fun. Staff meetings, though, needed help. They were a time to reflect on the past month and give each other a chance to speak our minds, which everyone, for the most part, felt comfortable doing. There were a few who never said anything and would just listen, so I tried to use their body language as a barometer for how they felt about the topic being discussed. But I couldn't quite read it, of course—I would just assume I knew what was going on in their heads. And I was not ready to ask what was really going on with them.

Describe a time that your body language was misread by someone:

How did you respond?

Describe the outcome:

How do you want to present yourself to other people?

What is one thing you can do this week to make that happen?

At these once-a-month meetings we ate snacks, announced the top performers, talked about what was coming up, and decided what the class would be for the next month. We would then discuss anything that wasn't going well in the salon.

One positive thing we did was set up a new way of finding solutions to problems in the salon. When someone would bring up a problem we were having at a staff meeting, we would have a group conversation to find a solution. As manager, I would drive the discussion, but the

Chapter Nine: Staff Meetings

whole staff would offer solutions. We would decide on a trial solution, and then put a time frame on trying the new idea. And that was the final decision, no discussing it until the end of the trial period. I discovered later this was one of the key pieces to the communication puzzle that held us together. It allowed us to *try on* change, because we had an end point if we didn't like it. And if it worked, we could just keep going! It would later help bring us to an all-time-high performance.

Trying incremental changes while knowing there was an end if it wasn't the right fit allowed us to try lots of new solutions, and eventually discover ones that would work for everyone.

Describe some solutions that have created positive change in your salon:

Describe how you feel when positive change is implemented?

What is your role in these changes?

STAFF MEETING EXERCISES

Use this worksheet to consider different ways in which you can change the staff meetings in your salon. How can you tweak the process to be more inclusive of the entire staff's opinions on both problems and solutions? How can you stay flexible with your decisions so that if something isn't working, the team can adjust and find the *right* solution? Answer these questions to find the best solution for your salon.

How do staff members bring up challenges in the salon?

Who generally offers solutions to the challenges presented?

How do you decide which solutions to try?

What would need to change to have all staff members included in the process?

Chapter Nine: Staff Meetings

When do you follow up on how a solution is working?

How do you determine if a solution is working?

Who communicates the success of the solution to the rest of the staff?

How do you determine if a solution is not working?

Who communicates the challenges of the solution to the rest of the staff?

What is your new plan for problem solving in staff meetings?

Meanwhile, as all of this was going on, I was still traveling one to two weeks a month, training stylists, working on photo shoots, facilitating large training events, and meeting managers and stylists from all over the country. It was inspiring to meet so many different people with incredible ideas and stories. In conversations, I started to notice the striking similarity of the "problems" they were all experiencing in their salons: high turn over, complaining stylists, disengaged staff, and low client retention. How was it possible that everyone across the country was having the same problems at work?

The more I traveled and got to know other salon leaders around the country, the more I learned about conducting staff meetings and facilitating communication between staff members. I started realizing that there were many different possible approaches to communication between management and staff. And some of the examples I ran across were not very successful. I had opportunity to see both effective and ineffective strategies from the outside.

Often, it was what I learned *not* to do that made the biggest impact on my own behavior. There were times I would listen to another manager speak of a problem in her salon, and think, Oh my. I have seen that problem in my own salon, and I do *not* want to sound like her. The thing is, those leaders were not necessarily doing anything wrong. They were doing the best they knew how to do.

During my travels, I heard so many amazing ideas for solutions from stylists and leaders that were simply not

Chapter Nine: Staff Meetings

being heeded, or else not put into motion; ideas from all levels of stylists—from apprentices to 20-year industry vets, educators to students. Everyone had ideas to contribute.

From exposure to all of these different stylists and their solutions, I realized that successful communication in staff meetings comes down to discovering a way to air all of the problems in a salon, and then finding a method of getting input from everyone for potential solutions. For us, it helped to put a time limit on trial solutions, at which point we checked in on how the solution was working and moved on from there. Contributions by all staff members create sustainability.

Chapter Ten:
Quarterly Reviews

Next up for serious change in the salon was the review process. During my first year as manager of the salon, I had instituted a basic quarterly review. In meetings with individual stylists, I had focused on what the stylist was doing *wrong* and what needed work, never really discussing what was going well.

Sometimes it would get pretty emotional. If someone would cry or become upset, it was too much for me to handle. I didn't want to know what the crying was about. I would shut down and hand that person over to my assistant. Christy was much more empathetic than I was; she could handle someone in that state of mind, and she could actually hear what the person was saying in that emotional moment—whereas I would get flustered. But when someone was angry, I would immediately step in and go toe-to-toe, puffing myself up and speaking in a way that would calm that person down. That was an important skill, but I still could not hear where their anger was coming from. I was good at controlling situations, but not fully understanding them. Christy, on the other hand, would have the opposite reaction; at the first sign of anger, she would shut down. After watching our opposite reactions for a few years, I wondered: how do I become a little more like her, while still retaining my ability to handle angry employees? I admired her ability to handle other people's emotions when they were not based in anger.

Who is someone you admire, and why?

How does that admiration influence actions you take in your own life?

What qualities about yourself do you admire most?

When we had made it to the end of a review, in an attempt to appear as though we were all on the same page, Christy and I would ask if there was anything we could do differently as managers. Of course, in that atmosphere of intense fear and scrutiny, there was rarely a response. If some brave soul had a suggestion, we said we would "consider" it.

Chapter Ten: Quarterly Reviews

Three years in, we were ready to focus on what employees were doing wrong *and* what they were doing right. I was also beginning to see that balance between work life and home life can be a big part of the motivation to achieve financial goals at the salon. People want to strike that balance, and they are much more reasonable about changing work hours when they feel they are being heard. It is possible to reach a compromise if you are open to what each person values.

In order to reach that compromise, managers must have a balanced understanding of what they need from each employee, and in turn, each employee must understand how much time off he or she needs to accomplish goals, as well as the real cost of that experience both to themselves and the salon.

I still had a hard time with this concept, even though I knew it would help the stylists feel better understood. I am not a "kid person," so when the topic of kids came up, I had a hard time with not judging the situation as "Oh, here we go again—you need time off for your kids!"

But let's face it: People *do* need time off for their kids, and of course it is extremely important to them. Who am I to say it shouldn't be important? Who am I to stifle their life *outside* of work in order to benefit mine *at* work?

For example: Sally is a team player. She knows her goals (inside and outside of work), the goals of the salon, and her responsibility to both. She needs time off for her daughter's soccer game and she is also aware that in order to get the new car she wants she needs to hit a certain goal at work. So she knows she needs to work another day or extra hours to achieve both the time off and the monetary goal. When open communication exists around personal and professional goals both parties, employee and leaders, can hold each other accountable for achieving those goals. That is when you begin to work with—and not against—each other. It is harder to rebel when we feel understood.

How do you currently set goals for yourself?

What makes setting goals important to you?

How do you hold yourself accountable for reaching your goals?

It is critical to find out what personal goals employees have set for their own success. What do they think needs

Chapter Ten: Quarterly Reviews

improvement in their own performance? I found it was much more effective to ask the stylists these questions then to tell them what I thought. I would offer my opinion, but the interesting thing was they usually beat me to the same points anyway. All I had to do was acknowledge their awareness, which by itself is empowering to hear.

QUESTIONS FOR QUARTERLY REVIEWS

Use these questions to help facilitate the quarterly review process. It may sound simple, but just listening to what your employees have to say about goals they have set for their own success both personally and professionally is a key element to management. If it is applied consistently in the review process, it will be the part of management that sustains successful goal setting.

In what areas do you feel you did well this month?

In what areas do you feel need improvement?

Describe your goals for next month:

What steps are needed to achieve those goals?

What are your goals outside of work?

How do your goals outside of work relate to your goals at work?

How do your goals at work relate to your goals outside of work?

Chapter Ten: Quarterly Reviews

At first, some of them didn't even know what to say. Their experience up to that point with reviews was this: Sit down across from your boss, listen to her rant about what you need to do better, and then get back to work. Maybe you were given a small token "congratulations!" if you had done something well that quarter, but the majority of the review consisted of management telling you what you were doing wrong.

Listening more carefully meant learning more about the stylists' real hopes and dreams. I had to put a lot of my own judgments aside to hear what other people were saying. I learned that people would only tap their potential when motivation coincides with their own values. I had to *hear* what my employees' professional and personal goals were. I needed to find out what they valued. Kids? Travel? Money? Down time? There is a tendency to think that if other peoples' values are not the same as ours, they are not as important as ours.

When going through a review, as a manager you don't have to agree with another person's version of what he or she wants out of life. I know that may sound strange to point out, but we tend to judge others' motivations if they are different from ours. The magic happens when we focus on what it is *we* desire, and then become curious but *not judgmental* about what *others* want.

As simple as it sounds, I have found that just listening to what your employees have to say about goals they have set for their own success both personally and professionally is a key element to management. Setting and achieving goals complicate the relationships between a salon leader, stylist and teammates. But one thing that is true, whether there is complete synchronicity or intense friction in these relationships: A team can and should work together to align and respect individual goals and values. In doing so, you will form an environment where everyone feels heard and respected. In turn, that will maximize the motivation, engagement and effectiveness of everyone involved. When everyone is working in tandem, it will create one of the most unstoppable businesses you will ever see.

Chapter Eleven:
Hearing vs. Listening

After we starting making serious changes to the review process, we wanted to expand it by creating a Goal Book for every stylist. The idea wasn't a new one; it originally came from my mentor Gordon. Each person would fill out daily and weekly goals, and then bring it to the quarterly review. The Goal Book became the jumping-off point for a more in-depth conversation about where an employee was in terms of creating his or her own work-life balance. I would expand on what we talked about by asking the questions I've written down on the Quarterly Review Exercises.

In the beginning, some stylists needed a little more prompting than others. Many had never been given the freedom to answer these questions by themselves in this kind of setting. But I was happy to do it because I wanted to know what they really thought.

Listening to someone's needs and *hearing* someone's needs are two different things, and at first I didn't have the awareness to notice the difference between the two. Don't get me wrong—I cared deeply about what every employee wanted to tell me. Just listening, I could pluck out the things the stylists said that fit what *I wanted* to hear, but not what *they needed* me to hear.

When you actually want to know the answer to a

question you are asking, there is a difference in the way your questions comes across to the other person. There is a difference in your voice and body language that shows you are paying attention to what the other person has to say. We have all been there and can sense the difference. Doesn't it feel so much better when someone is really paying attention to what you're saying?

Asking the right questions and truly *hearing* the answers will set you on the path to great communication.

Christy was great at hearing the answers. And as I said earlier, she could also handle a crying employee in a way I couldn't. I realized that I needed to expand my capacity to react in an appropriate manner to all emotional behaviors in the salon. I knew I had to step up. I needed to go outside of my comfort zone, to an uncomfortable place in my own head. I could not keep doing what I'd been doing my whole life and also change into a person who could handle a crying employee.

I knew from watching and talking to Christy that listening more closely to team members was the key, and I knew had to expand it past the staff meetings and quarterly reviews. I called a meeting for the sole purpose of hearing more from my employees individually. At that meeting, I made an announcement: "I am open to hearing what any employee thinks is not going well in the salon. But if you have a complaint, you also have to have a solution before approaching us with it."

We thought it was a great middle ground. Employees knew they could come to me with their problems at

Chapter Eleven: Hearing vs. Listening

any time, however I was not inundated with every single problem in the salon. They would either come to me with a solution we could work with, or they would think about it deeper before approaching me. Employees often found that their problems weren't as big of a deal as they had imagined.

This policy got all team members to reflect on what was bothering them. It was unbelievable how many issues resolved themselves, now that employees were given the power to make decisions and to come up with solutions. In fact, their solutions were usually better than the ones I would have come up with!

The only problem was that not all staff members felt comfortable coming forward with their problems. By implementing this policy, I continued to isolate the staff members that were too afraid to speak up or felt too much pressure to be perfect in their solution. These employees would just "deal" with problems they were having rather than going through a difficult discussion. After all, not everyone has an easy time coming up with solutions to problems. I should have been asking questions to support employees who had a hard time speaking up. Take a look at the Supporting Questions Exercise for examples of questions I could have asked to help less vocal team members talk about what was on their minds.

SUPPORTING QUESTIONS EXERCISE

Use these questions to help get a conversation going with less vocal team members. The more everyone feels heard, the more likely everyone is to talk about the substance of what is really going on. This can be used in conversations between team leaders and staff, or between teammates.

Describe what makes you feel the most successful:

Describe a challenge you are currently experiencing at work:

What does a positive change to this challenge look like?

Describe your role in that change:

When would you like to see this change take place?

What can be done this week to begin implementing this change?

These questions would have allowed them to say out loud what they needed from me as their leader. Most problems seem to lose their negative weight when they are said aloud. It's the manager's ability to guide a conversation that gets it to that place.

Even though it wasn't perfect, I had started to make positive change: opening the door of communication to all employees at all times, and empowering them to come up with their own solutions to problems. Those who *can* come to you with solutions, *will*. If I had just taken it upon myself to ask the right questions to the ones who needed a little help to see that they knew the solutions all along—that would have truly paved the road to success.

That said, even by opening up this small window of awareness, we improved our communication process dramatically. We could now have real discussions about what they wanted and how they could get there. I was no longer just telling them what to do. We were finally working together.

It's not always about big gains; making small, incremental changes can lead to the biggest successes of all. These small changes, both within each individual and as part of the greater whole of the salon, can foster an atmosphere of respect. The process begins to feel less like work and more like teamwork. This is one of the reasons why I'm now educating salon professionals on how to create unstoppable team chemistry through dynamic communication. Knowing the foundational information behind good communication is imperative. If you can achieve both high-level technical knowledge and clear communication among your salon team, I can't even begin to tell you the success you will experience. And the success will not limit itself to your salon; it will appear in the rest of your life as well. Just think about it: The stress of your work life will not flow over into everything you do, instead the success of it will.

Describe your vision for your career:

What steps will you take to achieve that vision?

What factors motivate your vision?

Chapter Twelve:
Acknowledgment

At this point in year three, we were in a great place. Staff meetings were going well, the review process was ironed out and functioning, and we were all beginning to truly communicate with each other. But there was one hurdle left. It was my biggest pet peeve.

It all came down to one word: Acknowledgment. By acknowledgement, I mean going out of my way to praise an employee for doing his or her job. I don't mean the big moments, I think we all know that it is important to recognize a team member for doing an outstanding job. I'm talking about just going out of our way to say, "Hey, great consultation," or "That was a beautiful color." Even a small kindness that shows you are paying attention, like "I love that you are very particular and thoughtful about how you put the magazines away at the end of the day. It really helps make it look great in here." Acknowledging our teammates' successes that we have all day long.

I hated the thought of acknowledging someone for what I considered to be just doing his or her job in an acceptable way. The idea of it actually had a physical effect on me. I would begin to feel so uncomfortable and angry, even at the smallest thought of it. Why did I need to pat someone on the back just for showing up to work? I didn't get it.

That is, until our company hired Gallup to poll all employees. Thousands of stylists and managers surveyed, and the number one thing that people wanted more of? Acknowledgment. You could not deny the importance in recognizing individual accomplishments. It was right there in black and white.

When I found that out, it was as if the leadership gods were playing some kind of sick joke on me. I mean, I had already been opening up to the team and letting them have a say in things. I really had to acknowledge the small things, too? Wasn't I acknowledging them just by letting them have a say in the first place? Oh, for crying out loud, I thought. Fine, let's do some acknowledging.

It started off by placing paper stars on the wall in the back room, and encouraging the staff to write on them, saying something nice about someone else in the salon. It was anonymous in order to focus on the comment itself rather than who said it. Some people liked it—they finally felt like others understood how hard they were working, and it was all right out there in the open for the world to see. Others did not care for it at all.

I began to try different approaches. I'm just experimenting, I kept thinking. Nothing wrong with that—I'm not tied down to permanently changing my ways. In meetings, I would have a stylist come to the front of the group and get praised for something good he or she had done. Again, some people loved it and some people hated it.

Great, I thought. There isn't one solution that

Chapter Twelve: Acknowledgment

everyone likes. Now I have to come up with different ways to do this stupid acknowledging thing? I just kept reminding myself that it was an experiment, and I was doing this exercise mostly to prove that it wouldn't change anything.

For the stylists who didn't like to be called to the front of the room, I had to come up with something more personal and private. I started leaving notes on their stations or at the computer for them to see when they clocked in. Most people enjoyed the notes, but some thought they were just a cheap cop-out.

In any event, I was learning fast. Everyone seemed to like being acknowledged in a different way. It's an easy realization now, but this idea ran completely opposed to what I was taught my whole life. I always believed that in a business setting, everyone needed to be treated the same. Isn't everyone equal?

ACKNOWLEDGEMENT EXERCISE

Use this worksheet as a starting point for a conversation about how all staff members like to be acknowledged in the salon. Think of ways you could use this exercise as a group activity.

For stylists:
How do you like to be acknowledged for your contributions to the salon?

Describe how it changes your level of engagement when you are acknowledged:

Describe how you acknowledge others around you?

What are you currently doing to acknowledge employee or coworker contributions in the salon?

List new strategies you can do to show appreciation for teammates:

Chapter Twelve: Acknowledgment

This realization brought everything together for me. I did not need to treat everyone the same because not everyone needed or wanted to be treated the same. I also began to understand that in addition to personal goals for things like money, time off, and problems in the salon, everyone had his or her own goals and aspirations for roles *in the salon*.

So many tasks need to get done every day to run a salon properly. Duties like doing the color inventory, ordering retail, and creating schedules, among many others. I realized that I had been assigning these responsibilities to team members without considering their goals. Of course, we all have to do some things we don't like at work. That is part of everyone's job in every industry. However, I had a lot of incredible talent that I wasn't using to its full potential.

In order to find the tasks the team members liked to do, and *would* do consistently, I just had to ask them what they wanted to do. Everyone knew his or her own answer. This idea was so simple, it had been right in front of me the whole time.

In addition, I knew what each person's strengths were from a manager's viewpoint. I just hadn't thought of assigning tasks according to what people might actually want to do. So with their individual wants and needs combined with my knowledge of their strengths, we came up with the perfect role for each employee.

The best part is, it is much easier to give praise and acknowledgement to someone who is doing a job or task they *want* to be doing, because most likely they will naturally be doing a good job.

Chapter Thirteen:
Vision, Mission, Values

The salon was moving along. We were communicating more effectively than we ever had before. All team members felt like their work meant something. I was feeling pretty good about where we were. So what was next? Time to think about the business as a whole. We needed to fully explore what our culture as a team was.

In any business there is a vision, a mission, and a set of values that determines the culture of the organization. I'm sure you've already heard these terms. Some businesses may not have defined them yet, but they are still there. These elements combine to shape the culture of a salon. If they are not clarified to all members of the team, drama tends to fill in the gaps of the culture. Here is a basic definition of these elements:

Vision: This statement should inspire you and give direction to your business. It describes what you want your business to be, and how do you see it working five, ten, or twenty years from now. Dream big!

Mission: Why does your business exist? The mission statement will explain the purpose behind your business and how it will be communicated to both clients and employees.

Values: What are you doing this for? This statement describes what your motivation is and what you believe is the foundation of success for both yourself and your team.

In our salon, we all had a general idea of what our vision, mission, and values were. We had discussed them at length in the past, but had never examined whether or not our actions were connecting to our thoughts. Were we really walking the talk?

We decided to call a special staff meeting to do just that.

What we had come up with in the past was the following statement:

The main focus and foundation of our salon is education. This direction enables us to surpass clients' expectations and create an environment where clients and staff feel welcome and accommodated.

It was all coming together. It was now time to define what the *stylists'* missions were. What were *their* visions? What did *they* value? How did each person want to contribute, and what did he or she want in a work place and a clientele? Otherwise, it was only what the people running the business needed. And can the people running the business ignore the visions of our employees; their values and what they want to accomplish? I had already scratched the surface of this idea and was starting to ask these questions—only now my hearing was improving!

VISION, MISSION, AND VALUES EXERCISE

Use this space to work on your vision, mission, and values statements. Think about the reflection questions you've answered so far, and what the answers mean for your salon or yourself. You don't have to have fully formed statements just yet, use this space to get all of your ideas down.

Vision

Describe what your business is:

Describe what achievements you see for yourself or your business in the future...
In one year:

In five years:

In ten years:

What are the big dreams you want to accomplish?

Who are your clients, and what do you hope to offer them as a business?

Mission

Describe why your business exists:

Describe how you want clients to see you or your business:

Describe what you will focus on to achieve these goals:

Values

Describe what motivates your vision:

At your core what do you believe is the foundation of success... For yourself?

For your team?

Describe what you do right now that is aligned with these values:

Describe what is not currently aligned with these values:

Describe how you will stay aligned with these values in the future:

This idea, the power of discovering every single employee's vision for his or her own life and using it to push the business forward, is something I now know we had only begun to harness. It is the salon dynamic I thought about most after I stopped managing. Only now do I truly know how successful we could have been. We were so close to finding this alignment; I just needed to step back to be able to see it.

Team alignment and chemistry are born out of understanding each individual team member's vision, mission, and values. The group goal then becomes about meeting and fulfilling each other's needs, not just that of one individual. In one-sided relationships, the unheard party will ultimately leave to pursue personal goals. But when balance is achieved through open communication, a team that will stand the test of time is formed.

Only when you know what you want and are striving for on an individual level can you be on the same page with everything going on in your work: the business, your boss, and your team members. When you establish what it is that *you* want, you can find fellow team members with matching values. Whether you are hiring an employee or are the one looking for a position at a salon, when you know what is important to you, you can find—or form—a group of people whose personal visions can be mutually understood and respected. Your mission will follow a path that is in sync with the people around you. You and your coworkers will work together toward both individual and shared goals. That feeling of fighting for what you want will become a feeling of working together to *create* what you want. A mutual respect between team members (and for the business) forms, and that is the glue that holds any business together. It pushes both the salon and the individuals alike to reach their full potentials.

Chapter Fourteen:
Leaving the Company

You know that moment when you feel completely at peace with how things are going and suddenly everything changes? The universe decides, no no, little grasshopper, you are not done yet...

At about this time in my tenure at the salon, I heard my mentor and boss Gordon was retiring within a year. I started crying when I heard the news—no joke. I was on set filming a training video. Filming was about to begin when a close friend and co-worker of mine asked, "Did you get Gordon's voicemail?" I said, "No." "Oh, so you don't know he announced his retirement?"

It was as if my whole career came to a screeching halt. He was the reason I worked for this company. His vision, his mission, and his values kept me motivated and fostered my connection.

My next year became about preparing for my mentor to retire. I was thrown into chaos. I did not know how to respond to it. I was upset, and all I could do was try to figure out what was keeping me at the salon. Don't get me wrong, the staff was a huge part of it, but I felt like Gordon's vision was what was driving me to strive for my teammates. I felt like the center of my work-self was falling away.

I understood the culture we had created in our salon. We had mapped out how we worked as a team and what we stood for very carefully by this point, and I loved and appreciated the team. But what about the company I worked for? I did not know what *its* vision was. I did not know what the company stood for, and I sure did not know how they were going to make that clear. I knew and understood my mentor, but with him gone...what *was* this place?

I would spend the next year trying to find out. I would attend meeting after meeting with upper management and marketing, trying to get a better idea of what they were doing and what their insights were on what was going on in "the field," as we individual salons were known.

Keep in mind: I was invited to these meetings. In theory, they wanted to hear from us. They wanted to know what was happening in individual salons like ours, which sounded great to me. I kept telling myself, "This is going to be OK; they are open to hearing what I have to say."

When someone is out of touch, good intentions can only go so far. Sound familiar? What was happening here was exactly what I had been doing earlier with my teammates. You can have all the good intentions in the world, but when you are not willing to hear what your employees are saying and try to understand their concerns or visions, the interpersonal chemistry will never form. And eventually, as I mentioned before, we will look elsewhere to find that chemistry, or at least not be as productive and engaged as we all have the potential to be.

Chapter Fourteen: Leaving the Company

Deep down, I knew this was the beginning of the end for me with that company. I could not align myself with its mission and values. In fact, I could not see them clearly—period. And looking back, I think part of me didn't want to. I heard a voice speaking to me from deep down, telling me I had to make a move. I had gotten so far with this company, but the voice kept getting stronger. I was beginning to realize how much knowledge I had gained from all of the unforgettable experiences, friendships and discoveries. I could see my potential expanding; I knew I needed something more.

What is your true potential?

What is one thing you can do this week to explore your potential?

I had to decide whether to stay with this incredible team we had created or follow my inner voice. I realized that if I were to stay and push this feeling down, I would begin to resent everyone around me. Not because they were doing anything wrong, but because I knew I needed more outside experiences to further open my mind and widen my perspective. I felt the fear of turning out the way I saw the former manager I had replaced at the salon so long ago: burned out, not interested in new information, and resentful of everyone around me.

I had reached the limit of my current ability. I was deep in self-reflective mode, and I didn't know how to go any deeper. I knew I had another purpose; that I had much more to do. It was time to find out what that purpose was. I had found faith in myself. I knew who I was becoming and what I believed in. Everything I am always looking for is right here inside of me. I was becoming aware of—and connected to—my own vision, mission, and values.

On a scale of 1-10 (1 being not connected at all, and 10 being completely connected) how connected are you to your vision, mission, and values?

1 - 2 - 3 - 4 - 5 - 6 - 7 - 8 - 9 - 10

What allowed you to get there?

Chapter Fourteen: Leaving the Company 103

What will it take to get you higher?

If you're at a 10, what's next?

Chapter Fifteen:
New York City

It didn't take much to decide what was next for me. I had always known where I would go if I ever left my current salon. I talked long and hard with friends and family about moving, and it was not an easy decision. But I had a path. I knew where I could work and where I wanted to be, and that was New York City. I had spent the last five years working on photo shoots every few months in New York, and I had fallen in love. I knew I would live there at some point. I knew something was waiting for me there. So after many conversations, and pro- and con-lists, I decided to take the leap.

I was able to secure a wonderful life-changing position at a well-known salon in Soho. It was my number one job prospect from the beginning. I started working in late summer. And when I say working, I mean working!

I was the newbie once again. I even had to change my name this time; there was already a Renee working at the salon. At first I thought it would be fun. I mean new city, new job—why not a new name? I ended up choosing my middle name, Michelle.

I was starting over again: a student one day a week, an assistant another day, and a new stylist the other three days a week. Starting at a new salon after being somewhere for years—including many as manager—is no easy task. I felt like the wind was taken right out of me. No one knew who I was and where I came from. I was just a new girl—what did *I* know? I was about to experience karma from all of the old, bad ways I treated my employees. Luckily, I also got some of the good.

At the salon, I was fortunate to train under one of the most committed educators I have ever met. She managed to balance strict sternness with a smile that said, "You know I don't really mean it." She had a rare ability to make me understand the importance of what she was telling me, while never being condescending or mean.

The manager of the salon embodied the kind of manager I wanted to be. We talked about management styles, and she told me that she saw her job as helping her employees in any way she could to see their potential. That way of thinking is so in line with how I view management, and I respected her so much.

While management was everything I hoped it could be, the other stylists were a mixed bag. I experienced the evil eye right from the beginning. I had a lot of admiration for one of the senior stylists. I had watched and admired her in videos prior to starting at the salon. That is, until my first day when I walked up to her and introduced myself. I told her I loved her videos and her cutting style, and I was met with a cold reply: no expression, and just one lukewarm word: "Tha....nks."

Okay...I thought as I walked away. Did I just approach the wrong person? Wasn't she in the video? Did I make a mistake of some kind? She must not know what I was talking about.

Chapter Fifteen: New York City

The next piece to my karmic puzzle was that I had to find five models a week. This should not be hard, right? I'm in New York City, for Pete's sake. There are eight million people here! Well yes, that's true. But these people do not want to talk to you, or have the time to stop mid-stride on a subway platform and hear that they have to take two hours out of a busy day to come in for a haircut.

I began to lose confidence. I asked myself, "Can I really do this??" over and over again. To make matters worse, when I *could* find models, they often wouldn't show up to their appointment. Then it looked like I was incompetent and couldn't hack it.

Sound familiar? It was all an echo of the early days of the education program I implemented at my old salon. Only now, I was on the newbie side. I got to experience all of the awful things I had put my teammates through while I was learning to manage them.

It was such an obvious karmic payback that I began to see the humor in it. This was a part of what I was supposed to learn. I began to hunt for it; look for things or experiences that were familiar now that I was on the other side of the fence. I wanted to feel everything my old employees used to feel when I treated them in certain ways.

The first time I cut hair on the floor of the salon, I felt as if I was having an out-of-body experience. I felt like eyes were peering through the back of my head, and I didn't know where anything was. We did not have assigned stations, so you would carry around your tools and go to the first open station you saw. Often I would go to shampoo a client, and I would come back to the station only to find another stylist there cutting hair, having moved my things and set up with a client, using the station with no apologies.

"Well OK then, I guess that is the way it is done here," I kept telling myself. The whole thing created a situation of leading by bad example. You wanted a cape? Forget it. Trying to find a cape was like going on an Easter egg hunt. Was there one in the broom closet? The brush cupboard? Maybe hidden in a tool case or stuffed in a corner? If you were assisting the owner, you had better have one hidden somewhere it couldn't be found, along with a few clean towels, just in case.

Learning the ropes of a new salon is like nothing else. It is a giant competition to discern hierarchy and seniority.

Did I mention the very famous stylist, who was also now my boss, was working right next to me, or sometimes directly on the other side of the mirror from me? Shoulder-to-shoulder or eye-to-eye. No big deal.

When I finished my first haircut, I felt as if all the blood had left my body. I kept thinking, what is wrong with me? I have been on stage in front of hundreds of stylists. I'd been a lead stylist on photo shoots and training videos. I had also been the manager of a million-dollar salon. Why couldn't I get it together?

Unfortunately, this feeling would last for the next few months. I just could not make it go away. I felt very out of place. Yet something was telling me I just had to open my ears and eyes, I was supposed to be there. I have never felt so in and out of place at the same time.

Chapter Fifteen: New York City

Describe a time you felt out of place:

How did you end up in that place?

Describe how it made you feel:

Describe the thoughts you had about yourself:

How could you reframe that situation to serve you better?

Every day as I walked to work, I would say, "Get a hold of yourself!" I wanted this, right? Well, I loved the city. I loved being in it, just walking around made me feel the happiest that I can ever remember. I just love the energy there; I can never get enough. And I was so proud to be living there, proud of myself. I had always known it would happen, and there I was. So, this all had to mean something. I was there for a reason and I was going to find it!

Think about when you felt out of place. What did you discover about yourself in that moment?

I cried more in that first two months than I had in my life. I was being tested professionally and personally every single day. I am *not* a crier, and I did not let people or uncomfortable situations get to me. Michelle was letting me down at this point. Renee would have never cried or let others get to her. What was going on? Who was this person I was becoming?

Describe a time you did not recognize yourself, based on how you were reacting to a situation:

Chapter Fifteen: New York City

What did you learn about yourself in that moment?

How have you used what you discovered about yourself to motivate you?

I was discovering my softer side. But how could this be? I moved to New York City, the thick-skin capital of the world, and I was a blubbering mess. I always felt I belonged here *because* of my hard outer shell. Of course I always knew I had this softer side, I just never thought it would serve me well, so I never let her out. Was this what I was meant to move here for? No way could this be true, yet there she was every single day, popping up like an annoying little sister. What am I supposed to do now? How do I make this work? I'd become a softy in New York.

Some things were going well. My clients were fantastic. I expected these mean, demanding clients, and that was not the case at all. I really connected with them. The funny part to me was that I would receive notes on my tip envelope that said things like, "You are so sweet, thank you!" or "You are just so nice and sweet!" I would call my former employees and we would have a huge laugh over it! As you know by now, I was not known for being sweet and nice in my former position. So as funny and great as it was to be having people call me sweet and nice, it made me feel more out of place, and I did not know how that was going to help me navigate New York City.

I did get one big sign that I was on the right track: I found my New York City apartment on my first day of looking. I went with my broker to see a place at the north end of Manhattan in Washington Heights. We walked out of the subway into a tree-filled park, and I could feel the beautiful fall leaves crackling underneath on the early-September ground, smelling the delicious scent of real earth. I knew this was the place, it already smelled and felt like home. I love nature, and it felt comforting to smell the earth *and* enjoy city life, too. We walked down the wide sidewalks up to a 1930s-style building and took the elevator to the top floor. We walked into the apartment, and it was beautiful. It was so clearly the New York apartment of my dreams. Tons of sun with a normal-size bathroom and kitchen separate from the living space. It even had an entryway. All 400 square feet of it was perfect! I was in great spirits, and nothing was going to stop me from discovering whatever it was I was here to find.

When we follow our gut, life begins to open up, and challenges seem much less difficult. We end up having a hard time when we fight that feeling, telling ourselves that it's going to be too much work to get what we want, or

Chapter Fifteen: New York City

when we give in to self-doubt, fear, and worry of what others will think. When we get to that state, it's easy to feel overwhelmed and to shut out our intuition.

Honestly, it can be scary to listen to your gut. At times it can even seem like you're going crazy. You may think, "What am I doing? This can't be right, can it?" In that moment, listen closely. Your intuition may be telling you to move slowly and with caution, but you should still go with it, don't fight it. That voice is telling you your direction. It is telling you how strong you are and how much you can handle.

There have been times when my intuition has taken me to places that I never imagined; places that hurt me and seemed to me like the end of the world. How could my intuition have been "right" when it felt so bad? I have come to realize that I need to live through difficult times in order to move on to the next thing. I need to see what I am capable of handling, and also what I don't want to do or to be (which are just as important). We are capable of so much, some of which can expose an unknown side of our persona that may not be very flattering or align with our values. Those values will be recalled or revealed by the difficulties we face. I have become addicted to following my intuition. It gives me a rush and pushes me forward in a way that feels unstoppable.

Describe a time your intuition told you something was right, even though at the time things were not going so well:

Describe how it changed your perspective in that situation:

What was it about you that made you listen to your intuition?

Chapter Sixteen:
My New Client

A few months later, I was getting in to the swing of things. I had found a groove at work, and I was feeling better. Every so often, something would put me back in my shy and self-doubting phase. But trusting I was supposed to be on this path made me keep going.

And then it happened. One day at work, I walked up to the reception desk to get my next client. She was a petite woman who spoke quietly. She was not the usual type of person I would feel a connection to, but remember—my soft side had been exposed. She was meeting Michelle, not Renee! And I felt a connection to her right away. There was something about her that stood out to me.

We began our appointment and she told me about a business she was starting—a business as a life coach. I had no idea what a life coach was. I thought of them as useless and silly. Just tell people to buck up and figure their life out; how is that a career?

By the end of the appointment I was hanging on every word she said about life coaching. As she spoke and this new Michelle side of me listened (ahem, *heard*) what she was saying, I began to see what it was about. It was not about telling people how to figure their lives out. It was not like a sports coach telling you what to do. It was about helping people see that they already possess the answers to any "problem" they have. People just need a non-judgmental and unbiased space to think and talk out loud while being asked supportive and empowering questions about what it is they are trying to figure out, and they will come to their own conclusions.

HOLY. COW. It hit me like a ton of bricks. I had butterflies in my stomach. I knew: This was it. This is what I had been looking for. Everything I learned about human interactions over the years came swirling back to me. All the thoughts I had in the past of how I always saw my salon staff, but could never find a way to articulate. The way I saw so many salon leaders and their teams work or not work together. I had always been looking at what other people could do to make the environment better, looking for that new idea outside of myself. I did not own what it was I *myself* was capable of.

This was my purpose. I could use my experience to help other people by choosing a career I never knew existed. This is what I was there in that city to discover; it is why I had to discover my softer side, and why I met this wonderful person sitting in my chair.

Describe a time you felt a new part of you connected to a purpose:

Chapter Sixteen: My New Client

What action did you take after feeling that connection?

What has changed for you from taking that action?

After this revelation, I sat on the feeling for a bit. Think of what acting on it would mean: I would have to quit this amazing job opportunity that I was given, and how could I do that? I had been given a chance not a lot of people get. Furthermore I had now begun to travel and teach for this well-known company, a position I knew very well and was comfortable with. And then there was of course Gordon, the person I would do anything for professionally, who had helped me get this position. How could I disappoint him, too, and just throw it away? I began to second guess myself and think I was just being a wuss, just looking for a reason to get out of this job I liked, but did not love. There it was: that self-doubt we all deal with, telling ourselves we don't deserve what we want because of how it looks or what others will think.

I started to really examine how I was feeling at work. I had a strong sense that no one trusted each other or knew the "right" way to do anything in the salon. I didn't feel like anyone trusted our ability to figure out solutions to problems by ourselves. I constantly felt second-guessed or I was second-guessing myself—the two became blurred, and that shook my self-confidence. In the past I had challenged myself to excel out of pride and the knowledge that I had the ability to find the answer if I was curious. That part of me was gone.

It made me think back to when I was building self-confidence at my old salon, specifically under the direction of the manager who had preceded me. I realized that though I discovered I had drive and a knack for management, I had really no idea how hard it may have been for her just before she left. Who knows why it wasn't working as well as it could have at the salon. She could have been angry at something that had nothing to do with the salon: perhaps she felt looked over or didn't enjoy being a manager. Perhaps a simple perspective shift to staying curious about what was going on with *her* was all that was needed to help both her and the salon succeed.

Curiosity allows you to ask a question without fear of it being the "right one" or feeling like you are going to "sound stupid." Being curious takes guts, and it comes from within as well as from your environment. Your surroundings can challenge your ability to feel confident enough to express real curiosity.

I was lucky to have had an environment in my

Chapter Sixteen: My New Client

upbringing and in my early professional life that allowed for it. I attributed this powerful perspective to the influence of my father and Gordon. For example: Any time I "failed" at something I was never asked, "Why did you do that?" They would never dwell on the fact that something was even wrong. Sure, we would discuss what we thought went awry in order to see what I would do differently the next time, but it always just felt as if we were looking at the situation, examining it and not judging it. And the conversation inevitably led to the simple statement:

Well, do it again.

That's it: Do it again, the most powerful yet simple statement spoken by two of the most influential people in my life. Think about it, that statement left me with only two options. I could wallow in self-pity or do it one more time. Figure it out and thrive. Discovering you have the ability to learn anything you desire by not letting *one* so-called "failure" get in your way is life-altering. After all, we need the "failure" to get to the correct answer most of the time.

In this new environment, I experienced something I had never felt before. I was achieving goals out of fear and judgment. I had lost my "just do it again" mentality and my mind was clouded. It was debilitating, and I was beginning to feel myself go backwards.

Describe a time where you had to make a big decision regarding a career move:

What thoughts came up?

What, if any, limiting thoughts surfaced?

Describe the outcome:

Describe how this experience has empowered you:

Chapter Sixteen: My New Client

After three months, I had to reach out to this client again. I emailed her, asking if we could meet for coffee to further discuss what this coaching thing was. She agreed to meet. I was so excited; I could just feel the energy surging in me. I was coming up with so many questions and ideas. I wanted to talk to her about the things I thought sounded like coaching that I had already been doing, and how this could possibly be a new path for me.

As soon as she showed up in the coffee shop, we spoke as if we had known each other for a lifetime. Most of all, we talked about the idea of compassionate leadership, something I had never felt possible when I first began managing. Not until I had the experience of being a leader with my harder, more unforgiving side, and then discovering my softer, more connected side emerging did I realize they could come together to create something special. Something I felt was so unstoppable that I had to share it with everyone! I had discovered—finally—how to fuse my old assistant Christy's strengths with my own. And after all of my experience, I now knew how critical it was to make that transition happen.

This client, and new friend, Danielle Mehta, CEO and Creative Director at Danielle Mehta Branding, acknowledged what I was feeling was real and that coaching seemed like a good fit for me. That was all I needed. And there it was again—that gut feeling. I called up the training company, and signed up for the session beginning in November. At the time it was early June, and I had been in New York just shy of a year. It was all about to change again.

With this new beginning on the horizon, I had to figure out what my life was going to look like. Initially I thought I could work at the salon and work on my certification at the same time. Not long after I signed up for the November session, I realized keeping up the pace at a New York salon was not going to work with all of the training I had to complete. I began to think about a move back to Minnesota.

I was back and forth every second. One day I was going, the next I was staying—I would just have to find a less demanding salon job. But then an idea to move to northern California came up. A great friend of mine lived there, and we talked about opening a salon. I could complete the coaching certification in California since they held sessions there as well as in NYC. But something would be missing. Back home in Minnesota I had my family and a clientele I was sure I could rebuild quickly.

So I made the decision, I would go back to Minnesota where I would (hopefully) get my clients back. I could do my coach training from there, since most of it was online and over the phone. I could fly back to New York for the three intense in-person seminars we had to attend. It was an ideal set up.

The decision to move back home brought me back to thinking about the team and how we interacted during my last year as manager. A big part of our success was the fact that our communication had gotten to such a clear place it allowed us to make decisions and go with them quickly; we saw the benefits and possible challenges but

Chapter Sixteen: My New Client

we knew we could always work through them as they came up. We trusted each other. I had gotten to a true place of caring and compassion. I knew the things they wanted not only in their career, but also in their lives. It allowed us to get on the same page, to hear each other and to be patient with each other. It was the key to success I had always looked for, and it was already happening. I now possessed that same compassion for myself, knowing what I wanted not just out of my career but my personal life as well.

I had come to realize that we all have the opportunity to figure out what we want out of our environment, and then say it out-loud, manifesting it from within. And if we find that we are in a workplace that is not the right fit, we shouldn't second-guess our intuition. We must ignore any naysayers and trust our intuition. We need to see past all of the assumptions and false interpretations and create our own best conditions for success.

Chapter Seventeen:
Return Home

Since being back in Minnesota, I have realized how we as humans tend to react towards change. I've been asked so many times, "So, what really happened?" "Did you hate it?" "Was it too hard?" "It was too expensive, right?"

Why do we always think a major move or change is because of something bad? New York City was the best thing to ever happen to me. I discovered so many things I would like to do, as well as the simple fact that I *could* do them, and it was relatively easy for me. I gained a sense of flexibility and freedom I had not felt before. These feelings allowed me to understand how to listen to my intuition and how to choose what is best for me. It was liberating.

Listening to our intuition, talking about our dreams and goals in an authentic way, and being open to the same in others will allow us to communicate with ourselves, which allows for clearer communication with others. That will help us reach success not only at work, but also in whatever we see as the full potential of our lives.

Limiting ourselves due to fear of what others may think is a very difficult thing to escape. I have been learning this lesson from the earliest days of my career. After many years of consideration, and particularly after my time in New York, I came to understand that being aware of when it is happening and trying to tone down those negative thoughts is where the real work of listening and tuning into your intuition begins. It comes from daily practice. Every time I begin to feel insecure because I'm considering what someone may or may not be thinking of me, I think to myself: Why am I feeling this way? I know that this type of negative thought for me is triggered by having ideas about new ventures, doing something creative, or in some way putting my own ideas out there for the world to see. So in the end, I remind myself that these negative thoughts are actually something positive. These thoughts indicate that just below the surface of that thought, my intuition is speaking up, trying to tell me what I *should* be doing.

So really, why *can't* we think of that insecure voice as a positive thing? We do have the choice, since it's all in our heads. It sounds silly, but it works. You can begin to manifest more positive relationships because you are not reacting to others based on the stories you are making up in your head.

When do you notice that insecure voice being triggered?

How do you respond when this happens?

Chapter Seventeen: Return Home

If it holds you back: How could you respond in a way that is true to yourself?

I am now renting a chair in a beautiful salon in Minneapolis. Renting is a great way to gain freedom and flexibility, but what might we lose in terms of working to achieve a larger goal as part of a team? We must strive to transfer the flexibility and freedom of renting to a team salon situation. It all begins with us. No matter where you work, it is important to be clear and concise in your communication with others, as well as graceful and open about what you want and need. You can achieve that by hearing what others around you need, and knowing that it's most important to learn from the mistakes and still be kind to yourself. Learn your lesson and choose to move forward, or realize the lesson may take time to figure out but to move forward anyway, having faith the lesson will come to light at the right time.

We so often invent that negativity in our own heads, and then live according to it. We can allow it to take over our deepest desires, ignoring what we know in our hearts would make us fulfilled. We must choose openness and curiosity in our lives by not looking at what we did "wrong" as something not to do again, but by looking at what we learned to do *right* in a difficult situation. We must recognize what we discovered about ourselves that we would want to do again. Just that small shift in thinking will invite positivity into your life and begin to rid our minds of negative buildup. It is all a choice—choosing a positive or negative outlook is up to each individual. We cannot wait for others around us to change; we must take charge and choose a positive perspective for ourselves.

Trust me, I felt this was the biggest lie when I first began to change my thinking. But the changes in my life that have resulted from looking and focusing on the positive in ANY situation have been beyond all expectations. Life is just easier, there are more good things in my life, and I feel fulfilled.

It has been a long journey to my current place of understanding, and I know that this place is not static. It is constantly changing and evolving, being challenged because of the people I meet and the choices I make.

The journey is not magically over one morning, we don't just wake up and know ourselves and never evolve again. It is one of the gifts of life, to be able to change and grow, moving with life instead of against it. We must learn to find the grace to welcome our mistakes and learn from them, because nothing is perfect or exact. We must enjoy the character our soul has developed over the years.

Chapter Seventeen: Return Home

What are your biggest takeaways from this self-reflection journey?

How will you continue to practice your mindful makeover?

Acknowledgements

A very deep and special thank you to all of the people who helped make this book possible.

Thank you to my husband for always allowing me to be who I am, or who I am seeking to become, even with all of life's crazy twist and turns. To my mother Jean and all six of my siblings and their spouses, you always show so much excitement and support for my crazy endeavors, thank you for all of your support.

To my editor and lifeline through this process Emily Shetler, it's as if you sat in my brain, organized all of my thoughts, and placed them in order exactly how I envisioned them. Ben Adams, thank you for the second pair of editing eyes.

Milena Rose Ghattas and Jamie Wiley, thank you for being my industry sounding board, you are two stylists that have the industry at your fingertips, and your opinions mean the world to me. To my *entire* Regis family especially the MOA crew, we had the magic. From the bottom of my heart, thank you for opening yours. Christy Becker, Alex Farina, Maria DeVito Ascher, every day I strive to follow your lead. Thank you for including me on your journey. To Kathleen Savano (KAT), Terry Varty-Kaslow, and Carmel Lawless for the priceless technical skills and mentorship. To Eric Turnlund for showing me how to blow-dry, without that I would not have had the confidence to go on that first video shoot. To all of my clients, your enthusiasm and support not only humbles me everyday, but pushed me to complete this book...partially because I knew you would ask about it at you next appointment!

To my coach Danielle Mehta, meeting you changed my life, I found my voice through our sessions; this would not have been possible without you.

To my mentor Gordon Nelson, without you this story would not be what it is today. Thank you for always believing in me and giving me a chance to grow without judgment.

In Memory of
Denise K. Bertucci

CPSIA information can be obtained
at www.ICGtesting.com
Printed in the USA
FFOW05n1928230116